Table of Contents

1. A Jealous God — 11
2. Sin Brings Family Curses — 21
3. The Next Generation Pays the Price of Our Sins — 31
4. Generations Becoming More Wicked — 41
5. Parents Influence the Next Generation — 49
6. The Family Was Blessed — 59
7. Getting Out from Family Curses — 67
8. Blood Reverses All Curses — 75
9. Breaking the Family Curse of Noah — 83
10. Family Traditions or Generational Curses? — 91
11. Bitterness in Parents or Leaders—Curses — 97
12. Curse-Proof Your Home — 105

About This Book

Why? Why are there so many repeat behaviors and repeat sins in our families today? I need answers to why Grandpa molested his daughter, why Uncle molested his daughter, and so on down the line. And why did Grandpa make moonshine and drink himself to sleep each night and all his sons are drinkers as well? Will our kids be the same as Grandpa, Uncle, Dad, Mom, and others?

I taught a class in Nursing Ethics, which used *The Ministry of Healing* by Ellen White as the textbook. I was surprised to see how she saw that our children will be tempted or weakened by our sinful ways. Then I heard two sermons on television mentioning the same thing. I began to study and preach what Scripture teaches about generational sins and family curses.

When I read the book of Deuteronomy, chapter 27, I discovered that God was warning His people of the tribes of Israel to stay out of sin or the whole tribe would be cursed. We know that tribes consisted of family groups. Today our churches consist of family groups.

One summer evening, a young man came into my office and said, "I'm tired of living a life that is out of control." He shared with me that his dad and his grandpa were both warlocks. He was confused how he ended up in the dirty job of riding in a wild and dangerous motorcycle group. He said, "It's as if I have a spell on me to live this way." Later on, in praying with this young man, God revealed to him that there was a curse put on him by his father. The Holy Spirit brought back to his memory that his father had pronounced a vow, placing some kind of evil curse on him and his twin brother. Both brothers were into lifestyles that truly would make their dad and grandpa proud. However, God wants to stop all vows and family curses. I asked him, "Do you want blessings in your life? Do you want your children set free?" That got him—when I asked about his children.

When you place God first in your life, you will receive blessings upon blessings and your children will be blessed. But allow the devil to rule in your life, and you will lose your children in this earthly pit.

"Be sober, be vigilant: because your adversary the devil walks about like a roaring lion, seeking whom he may devour" (1 Peter 5:8, NKJV).

You know that the Bible tells us to "resist the devil and he will flee from you." If your parents resist the devil, he will flee from your house. As parents, we can show our children how to resist, and they will start their families also resisting the devil.

"Be sober, be vigilant; because your adversary the devil, as a roaring lion, walketh about, seeking whom he may devour: whom resist steadfast in the faith ... But the God of all grace, who hath called us unto His eternal glory by Christ Jesus ... To Him be glory and dominion forever and ever" (1 Peter 5:8–11).

We must resist the devil—spiritually, mentally, and physically. When we resist, we receive God's blessings. We must resist the enemy by faith that His blessings come upon us and continue to be poured out on our children and grandchildren for a thousand generations.

"Therefore know that the LORD your God, He is God, the faithful God who keeps covenant and mercy for a thousand generations with those who love Him and keep His commandments" (Deut. 7:9).

Will your children, grandchildren, or great-grandchildren be the next great spiritual leaders? I told this young man that if he didn't want his three boys to grow up living in sex, drugs, and evil surroundings, he had better turn to God and seek deliverance from his family's generational curses.

I tell you, too, dear reader, if you follow God—serving Him and others, living for Him, reading His Word, praying, witnessing, and keeping committed to the Lord

Jesus Christ—then your children and your grandchildren will mature in Christ and give Satan and his kingdom a rough time.

CHAPTER 1

A JEALOUS GOD

Do you remember Harry Chapin's song, "Cat's in the Cradle"? I used to sing it when I was a teenager.

The song was about a father's realization that his son had grown up just like him. The son had been cursed with the curse of the father. That curse was about not taking time for his son, and the son likewise didn't have time for the father.

Could we parents be placing curses on the characters of our children? Could we be allowing Satan to have his way with our precious young people? This book is a quick look at what could possibly be behind God's message, "For I, the LORD your God, am a jealous God, visiting the iniquity of the fathers upon the children to the third and fourth generations of those who hate Me" (Exod. 20:5, NKJV). My object in this book is for readers to take a look at families in Scripture and understand how family curses were passed down. We'll also take a look at my family curses and stories from my years of pastoring church families with their own family curses.

When we think of family curses (more commonly called "generational sins") we have to see that Scripture always gives us the good with the bad. On the good side of things, Scripture states—

"Therefore know that the LORD your God, He is God, the faithful God who keeps covenant and mercy for a thousand generations with those who love Him and keep His commandments" (Deut. 7:9, NKJV).

"Now it shall come to pass, if you diligently obey the voice of the LORD you God, to observe carefully all His commandments which I command you today, that the LORD your God will set you high above all nations of the earth. And all these blessings [and not curses] shall come upon you and overtake you, because you obey the voice of the LORD your God" (Deut. 28:1, 2, NKJV).

We also can look to Scripture for some of the more amazing words—sometimes sad words–about our families. Pay special attention to what it says about our children. "My people are destroyed for lack of knowledge. Because you have rejected knowledge, I also will reject you from being priest for Me. Because you have forgotten the law of your God, I also will forget your children" (Hosea 4:6, NKJV).

A Jealous God

"For I, the LORD your God, am a jealous God, visiting the iniquity of the fathers upon the children to the third and fourth generations of those who hate Me" (Exod. 20:5, NKJV).

It is our families that the devil wants to destroy and bring to complete destruction. His whole object is to bring down the priest of the house to get at the next generation, which is our children and then our grandchildren.

"For the land is defiled; therefore I visit the punishment of its iniquity upon it, and the land vomits out its inhabitants" (Lev. 18:25, NKJV).

The inhabitants are our children and their children. Do you want to be blessed? Do you want your next generation to be blessed? When we give God first place in our lives, we open our children to blessings upon blessings. When we play with sin, Satan has access to oppress our children.

> **WHEN WE PLAY WITH SIN, SATAN HAS ACCESS TO OPPRESS OUR CHILDREN.**

Satan was created as a perfect and holy angel who had great skills of organization and leadership and was capable of preciseness in his actions and plans. All these skills were for use in the kingdom of Heaven. He is now using these same skills to attack planet earth and all its inhabitants. Let us not forget that angels were made to be

God's army—to be very precise and orderly and knowing when, where, what, why, and how to bring blessings to God's kingdom. But now Satan uses all those skills to attack God. The best way to attack a home is at the level of the innocent and vulnerable child.

The angel Lucifer (who became Satan) knows and plans precisely when, how, and where to get to these precious ones. "All should understand that Satan was once an exalted angel. His rebellion shut him out of heaven, but did not destroy his powers and make him a beast. Since his fall he has turned his mighty strength against the government of heaven. He has been growing more artful, and has learned the most successful manner in which to come to the children of men with his temptations" (*Testimonies for the Church*, vol. 1, p. 342).

When I was a young boy, I remember many times hearing someone talking bad about my brothers, my sister, or me. If my father were around, anyone doing that had better be faster than a bullet. Nothing touched my father more than people bad mouthing his children, whether what they said was true or not. I have carried on that philosophy to some degree. I decided that I would not let Satan attack my children. I choose to bring blessings upon them by not giving place to the devil but, rather, by giving place to God in my life and claiming blessings instead of attacks from generational sins, which would lead to generational curses.

Could sin in our children be family sins that Satan claims rights to continue for generations? To answer, let's take a look at some verses in Deuteronomy.

"Moreover all these curses shall come upon you and pursue and overtake you, until you are destroyed, because you did not obey the voice of the LORD your God, to keep His commandments and His statutes which He commanded you. And they shall be upon you for a sign and a wonder, and on your descendants forever" (Deut. 28:45, 46, NKJV).

When the priest of the home—usually the father—carries sin, it allows Satan access to oppress our children in the same sinful areas as the father. Mothers who are living as a single parent and raising their children must stand with God as their priest, or their children will also produce their curses for another generation. "The fathers have eaten sour grapes and the children's teeth are set on edge" (Ezek. 18:2).

A few years ago, a 15 year-old girl came to me with this startling news, "Pastor Mitch, I'm pregnant and don't know how to tell my parents." I suggested she go home and ask her mother if her mother had been pregnant before she was married. The next day this girl told me that her mother had been pregnant before she was married, and her grandma had been pregnant and raised her first child for several years before meeting a young man that would marry her.

How can we break these curses or generational sins? I want families to know that curses can be stopped, and we can change our generation lines.

"And they overcame him by the blood of the Lamb, and by the word of their testimony" (Rev. 12:11).

"Christ has redeemed us from the curse of the law, having become a curse for us (for it is written, 'Cursed is everyone who hangs on a tree')" (Gal. 3:13).

If you (and especially if you are the priest of the home) follow God—serving Him, praying spiritual warfare, letting His word live in and through you—then you can claim your children and grandchildren, and they will grow up causing Satan to tremble at the testimony of your family.

A Man's Testimony

A tremendous wave of emotions overtook the thousands of men at the Georgia Dome. On the platform, keynote speaker Crawford Loritts struggled to maintain composure, attempting gracefully to receive a deafening five-minute standing ovation. He knew the cheers weren't for him. They were for the man to whom he had just delivered a heart-wrenching tribute—Crawford, Sr., the man's father, who lay on his deathbed five hundred miles away.

"He was a genuine promise keeper before there was a movement," the son told the arena full of strangers. He was the man who raised three kids with a firm hand, yet gave them freedom to choose, to make mistakes; he was the man who taught him what it was to be a man of his word. ("Men of Action," *Promise Keepers Quarterly Report*, January 1996).

I was amazed by Crawford's insight about what could be accomplished by the priest of the home. Was Satan seducing Eve to draw in the priest of the home, Adam, to be able to have access to the next generation? Was Satan trying to stop Cain and Abel from generational blessings? I believe so. Crawford's article in the *Promise Keepers Quarterly Report* had statements such as the following:

"My father's life was defined by integrity; he lived it, and passed it down to his children. He was the grandson of a God-fearing, uneducated slave named Peter. Crawford, Sr., was a generational by-product of a grandpa's undeterred devotion to family. For whatever reason," recalls Crawford, "through the word of God or prayer, something caused my great-grandfather to prioritize his family. Those values were passed down to my grandfather, then to my dad."

Three days after this speech, Crawford, Sr., died. The son spoke to the Georgia dome crowd, knowing full well he wouldn't see his father alive when he returned to his father's house. Crawford ends his article with another insightful statement:

"My great-grandfather … a slave in an abusive situation, found enduring hope in his relationship with Jesus Christ. Even though he never had a relationship with his own dad, he still put his family first. His faithfulness turned the tide for generations to come. It makes one wonder—what is preventing the men of our generation, with so many advantages, from becoming the first in a long line of godly men?"

Crawford Loritts' generations have shown that generations can be blessed for years to come.

"They overcame him by the blood of the Lamb, and by the word of their testimony" (Rev. 12:11).

CHAPTER 2

SIN BRINGS FAMILY CURSES

As I look back on my own life, I realize that some of the same things my grandfather was allowing in his life, my father was also allowing in his life. I never thought that down the years ahead I would be doing the same thing—just in a different place and in different ways, but, nonetheless, there were three generations of alcohol and sexual abusers.

As I have studied the generational sins of my family as well as those of my wife's family, I couldn't help but notice the newspaper account of Mickey Mantle's testimony. He told how his dad used to drag him around to pubs and bars, allowing him at a very young age to indulge, at times, in a few sips of beer. Mickey said that he did the same with his own three sons, and all three were in alcohol related rehab centers and on their way to recovery. All three generations were wrapped up in worldly lifestyles and drunkenness. In the article, Mickey confessed that he was sorry that he and his dad passed this practice on to their sons. Mickey also talked about his party lifestyle in the big leagues and how too much of his life was fixed on his Dad's pastime—alcohol.

Most Christians really want to follow the Word of the Lord, and they often ask God to show them their sinfulness. Maybe you're under a generational curse. Proverbs 26:2, NKJV, says: "… so a curse without cause shall not alight [come]." Sin is the cause of curses, and families allow Satan access to their children by opening the door of the family through sin.

God's writings warn us that a curse can be passed down from one family line to another (Exod. 20:3–6). I don't believe we are guilty of our parents, grandparents, or even great-grandparents' transgressions, but we all suffer the effects of their sinfulness if those sins are not dealt with. "It is written."

> **I DON'T BELIEVE WE ARE GUILTY OF OUR PARENTS, GRANDPARENTS, OR EVEN GREAT-GRANDPARENTS' TRANSGRESSIONS, BUT WE ALL SUFFER THE EFFECTS OF THEIR SINFULNESS IF THOSE SINS ARE NOT DEALT WITH.**

A Piece of My Story

My great-grandmother lived her life as one who was known for her attraction to bars and men. I would call her a bar-fly. Though I have few memories of her, there are family stories of her involvement with bars and other men. Since my grandfather was raised with this up-bringing, he also caught onto the bottle and had his own sexual misconduct. He was even known to have an attraction for little girls as well as adult women.

Could this pattern be passed on to my father and then passed on to me? Well, by the time I was seventeen, Satan had influenced me to go the same way. By the time I was eighteen, I was a full-time bartender who invited young ladies to sit at the bar to help my boss's liquor sales. I was already following my grandmother's curses, and now I allowed the curse to have hold of me.

At the age of eighteen, I had the opportunity to choose to go to a Christian college or play football at a local junior college. As I look back at the family curse, I should have run to the Christian college, but I wasn't in the Word of God, and the world's way was so much more inviting. How does a young eighteen-year-old not living at home go to school at 7:30 a.m., play football in the afternoon, and pay for his many needs? Well, it would have to be by a night job. So I got a job at a restaurant through my cousin, who set up an interview where she worked. Within months, my boss liked my work, and he mentioned that I could make much more money as a bartender with all the free tips from happy patrons. Soon I told him I was old enough to serve and sell liquor. He asked to see my I.D. I had just made a fake driver's license at my arts class at college, which showed my age to be nineteen, which was the legal age at that time. Satan had the curse ready to go down another generation. But God had not given up on someone breaking the curse of the fathers. My sins kept the curse alive and would have been threatening to my future children had not God continued to seek and save one who was lost.

I had an older brother who chose to go down the path of bars and women. Once he bragged to me that he had been able to drink a case of beer and still walk. Another time he bragged that, by the time of his twenty-first birthday, he would have slept with over 100 women. What really had my attention is that his son, who he hardly knew or was even around and is being raised by a stepfather, is turning out just like the father (my brother) whom he never knew. Is it accidental or could there really be a generational curse? Can darkness cause children to fall in the same areas that we have fallen? Doctors believe so.

Five months ago, I moved to a new church in a new conference and was required to have a complete physical evaluation to send in with my service records. I was awakened to the fact that even physicians see generational lines. When I filled out the insurance form and history questionnaire, both asked similar questions concerning my parents' and my grandparents' health. There were questions like, "Is there a history of heart disease in your family?" And the questions didn't stop there. Another question was, "Do any of your parents or grandparents have or have they ever had diabetes, arthritis, mental health problems, etc.?" *Doctors*, I thought, *must assume that, if previous generations have had these problems, the new patient could have them too.*

I recently heard a well-known minister on a Christian radio station mention that "many adopted children have ended up living lives like that of the parents they never knew." I'm beginning to believe that some of these children get their baggage from somewhere in the family line a few generations before their birth. Those who have adopted a child should know some background of the child and claim victory over their biological sinful traits or inheritance or curse of hereditary diseases.

"Dear Abby" Warns

Over the years I've been known to read a newspaper from cover to cover. I've been intrigued to see many of the letters that have been written to "Dear Abby" among other columnists. On the morning of April 8, 1997, I noticed in the local area newspaper the title of a "Dear Abby" column: "Ex-wife confirms her resolve not to return to abusive spouse." The letter writer mentioned how her ex-husband had emotionally and physically abused her and that her fifteen-year-old daughter lives with her while her seventeen-year-old son lives with her ex-husband. One day the ex-husband and son showed up, and she noticed that both her ex and her son laughed and ridiculed her about a letter she had taped to her mirror. The letter was from a lady who wrote to "Dear Abby" about how happy she was that she had gotten out of an abusive relationship. Here was Abby's response:

> Dear "Been There": I am gratified that "Goodbye Wife's" insight enabled you to resist the temptation to return to your abusive marriage. I'm concerned, however, that your son appears to be following in his father's footsteps. Please insist that he get into counseling to break the pattern that all too often is passed from one generation to another. He will be happier if he learns a better way to relate—with kindness and consideration for others.

The lady wrote her own letter to "Dear Abby":

> Dear Abby: The letter written by "Been There in Florida," the mother who was concerned that her son might inherit his father's abusiveness, was right on the money. I am a mother who stayed in an abusive marriage "for the sake of the children."

Finally, after twenty-three years, I left that marriage when I realized that my life was at stake. I left when the children went off to college, and I started over with no financial help from my ex-husband. I was still too emotionally involved to see the damage it had done to the children.

I now realize staying in the abusive marriage did not benefit my children. My son has spent time in prison for his aggressive behavior toward his girlfriend and now must attend anger management counseling for three years. My son and former husband are master manipulators. Both father and son can be charming, and then on a moment's notice and without any provocation turn into angry, aggressive, abusive monsters.

My daughter is afraid she will marry someone like her father. She has no faith in her ability to judge people; she doesn't stand up for herself and tends to minimize abusive behavior. She will do anything to keep the peace. Her low self-esteem is due to the abuse she received from her father and brother while she was growing up. Living in an abusive marriage is also very lonely. My definition of loneliness is being in the company of someone, yet feeling entirely alone because no intimacy exists.

I have now built a new life, and although it is filled with peace, tranquility, honesty and happiness, I'm sad to say it is without my son and the financial advantages I once had. We make our own quality of life when we leave an abusive situation. Perhaps it's not as comfortable financially, but it's far more gratifying, and definitely more peaceful.—LP

Dear LP: "Congratulations on having built a new life. Children benefit from living in an emotionally nourishing environment. It's easy to say that children need a two-parent household in order to become healthy adults; however, evidence has shown that children raised in an environment of tension, conflict and abuse often repeat these behaviors in adulthood, or become withdrawn and depressed and take on the role of victim."

The world is starting to see that curses do indeed come to us through the sins of the father or through the father *and* the mother.

CHAPTER 3

THE NEXT GENERATION PAYS THE PRICE OF OUR SINS

I'm seeing more and more of adults coming back to church and returning to the blood of the Lamb. When I ask them, "What kept you away so long?" they usually respond, "I just got bitter and I don't remember if it was at the pastor or the church or a member. I just remember that I got bitter and stayed bitter. But now I'm back asking God and His people to accept me." Then I usually ask, "How about your children? Are they serving God?" I have heard this response over and over again. "No, not at all, they are also bitter and have no interest in church life."

Let's look at two men who married and raised their children—one with God and the other without God. Max Jukes was an atheist who married a godless woman. In his line, we can trace 560 descendants: 310 died paupers; 150 became criminals—seven of them murderers; 100 were known to be drunkards; and more than half of the women were prostitutes. The descendants of Max Jukes cost the United States government more than $1.25 million in 19th century dollars.

Jonathan Edwards was a contemporary of Max Jukes. He was a committed Christian who gave God first place in his life. He married a godly young lady, and we can trace some 1,394 descendants: 295 graduated from college, of whom thirteen became college presidents and sixty-five became professors; thirty were judges; 100 were lawyers (one the dean of an outstanding law school); fifty-six became physicians (one the dean of a medical school); seventy-five became officers in the military; 100 were well-known missionaries, preachers, and prominent authors, while others were sent as ministers to foreign countries: three were elected as United States senators: three were state governors; another eighty held some form of public office, of whom three were mayors of large cities; one was the comptroller of the United States Treasury; and another was Vice President of the United States (https://1ref.us/mm01).

Of all the descendants who could be traced in the Edwards family, I don't believe that even one was a thorn in the flesh of the United States of America. We must follow God, being obedient to whatsoever He commands.

And God promises His people "a blessing, if ye obey the commandments of the Lord you God" (Deut. 11:27).

Several years ago, I was introduced by a pastor to his senior pastor. He introduced him as Pastor White. Pastor Charles White was senior pastor of the Paradise Seventh-day Adventist church in northern California. I wondered if he was related in any way to the Whites of the great Advent movement. I learned later that he was a direct descendent of Elder James and Ellen White. God has certainly continued to bless the James and Ellen White family.

When God is central to one's family, one can see the blessings continuing on from each generation to the next. When God says in Hosea that our children will suffer for our lack of knowledge, He wasn't kidding.

> **WHEN GOD SAYS IN HOSEA THAT OUR CHILDREN WILL SUFFER FOR OUR LACK OF KNOWLEDGE, HE WASN'T KIDDING.**

"My people are destroyed for lack of knowledge. Because you have rejected knowledge … because you have forgotten the law of your God, I also will forget your children" (Hosea 4:6, NKJV).

Satan Attacks Exactly and Precisely

A father came to me one day and asked, "Pastor Mitch, what can I do? I just busted my son smoking pot." I asked the father if he had ever smoked pot. He responded. "Yes, but it was years ago back in high school." When I asked if it was about the same age as the son was, he answered, somewhat taken back, "Well, yes, as a matter of fact it was also around my sophomore or junior year of high school." His son was in his summer vacation between his tenth and eleventh grades. I asked the man if his father was still alive, and would he ask him if *he* had ever smoked pot. The man answered, "Why, do you think he's got a problem?" I assured him I didn't think so, but I wondered if Satan had been attacking these three generations about the same time in their teen years. I found out weeks later that the man's father had indeed smoked pot a few times somewhere in his high school days. I also found out that the three generations of men were each the firstborn among their siblings. Maybe, dear reader, when sin enters the home, Satan has the preciseness to attack in familiar circumstances, if that has started in previous generations. I believe Satan is skillfully organized and works where he's allowed by the disobedience of fathers.

Remember, the devil is trying to put a curse on you. He wants an opening to be allowed to attack each generation in the same way he attacked the previous ones. Yet, we can respond, "I'm not under the curse of previous generations, I'm under the blood of Christ!" You can stop Satan by claiming victory in Christ. Claim the blood of Christ on your children that truly Christ on the cross took away any and all curses handed to your family from three or four generations back. On the other hand, if you give place to sin and allow generational curses to continue in your life, your children will be attacked seven times stronger and will be more likely to fall. In the next chapter, we will look at Matthew 12:43–45, where Matthew, I believe, is warning us that sin unconfessed in a home allows Satan rights of access to our children.

Let me share another encounter I had with a gentleman after I spoke on family cures. This man came to me with this story about his family line. He had been looking at some similarities between him and his dad. One was that they both were attracted to young women, even young teens. His father had had an affair in his late twenties with a thirteen-year-old girl. He also discovered that his grandfather had been in trouble with young teen and pre-teen girls. This man told me that his grandfather was in his late twenties when he was doing more than just talking to young girls. He went on to tell me that, when he was in his late twenties, he almost went to bed with a young thirteen-year-old. She was their babysitter and she was older looking and physically advanced. But that one evening, as things started to head in that direction, He cried out, "We can't! And I would like to ask God to forgive us and ask for His strength to overcome sinfulness." He believed God gave him victory right there. He said, "The forces of evil almost caused another generation to be cursed. But now I claim my children to be strong and able to continue this pattern of claiming the blood of Christ."

Let's look at a few statements on inheritance:

A certain man "should not have committed so great a crime as to bring into being children that reason must teach him would be diseased because they must receive a miserable legacy from their parents. They must have a bad inheritance transmitted to them. Their blood must be filled with scrofulous tumors [pertaining to tuberculosis of the lymphatic glands, especially those of the neck] from both parents, especially the father, whose habits have been such as to corrupt the blood and enervate his whole system. Not only must these poor children receive a scrofulous tendency in a double sense, but what is worse, they will bear the mental and moral deficiencies of the father, and the lack of noble independence, moral courage, and force in the mother.

"The world is already cursed by the increase of persons of this stamp, who must fall lower in the scale of physical, mental, and moral strength than their parents; for their condition and surroundings are not even as favorable as were those of their parents" (*Testimonies for the Church*, vol. 2, p. 379).

"The world is filled with men and women of this order [lustful passions]; and neat, tasty, yea, expensive houses contain a hell within. Imagine, if you can, what must be the offspring of such parents. Will not the children sink still lower in the scale: The parents give the stamp of character to their children therefore children that are born of these parents inherit from them qualities of mind which are of a low, base order" (ibid., p. 475).

"Vice in children is almost universal. Is there not a cause? Who have given them the stamp of character? May the Lord open the eyes of all to see that they are standing in slippery places!" (ibid., p. 477).

"I have been shown that Satan seeks to debase the minds of those who unite in marriage, that he may stamp his own hateful image upon their children. ... He can mold their posterity much more readily than he could the parents, for he can so control the minds of the parents that through them he may give his own stamp of character to their children" (ibid., p. 480).

Could we be allowing our children to be affected even while in the womb? Is it possible that what they feel, sense, hear, taste, touch, and think may cause them to be already claimed as children of the evil one? Most doctors agree that an unborn baby can feel, sense, and hear by about the sixth or seventh month of pregnancy. Things such as their parents' fighting or overeating, use of spices, drugs, alcohol, or tar and nicotine, and physical and emotional abuse can cause a child to be forever affected.

Satan is after our children from the moment of conception. The fear of rejection, thoughts of uncertainty, or hyperactivity can be instilled in a child from the womb. Diseased children are born every year because of the gratification of the parent's appetite. If a mother chooses to live as she pleases, or if a father is constantly bringing emotional abuse to the mother or even physical abuse, the child will automatically feel the same emotions at birth. The prosperity of any child depends on emotional, physical, and spiritual surroundings.

As this book is going to publication, a mother has just been arrested for murdering her child through tainted breast milk due to cocaine use while breastfeeding, and another mother is being tried for child neglect for her child's physical deformities due to drug use during pregnancy.

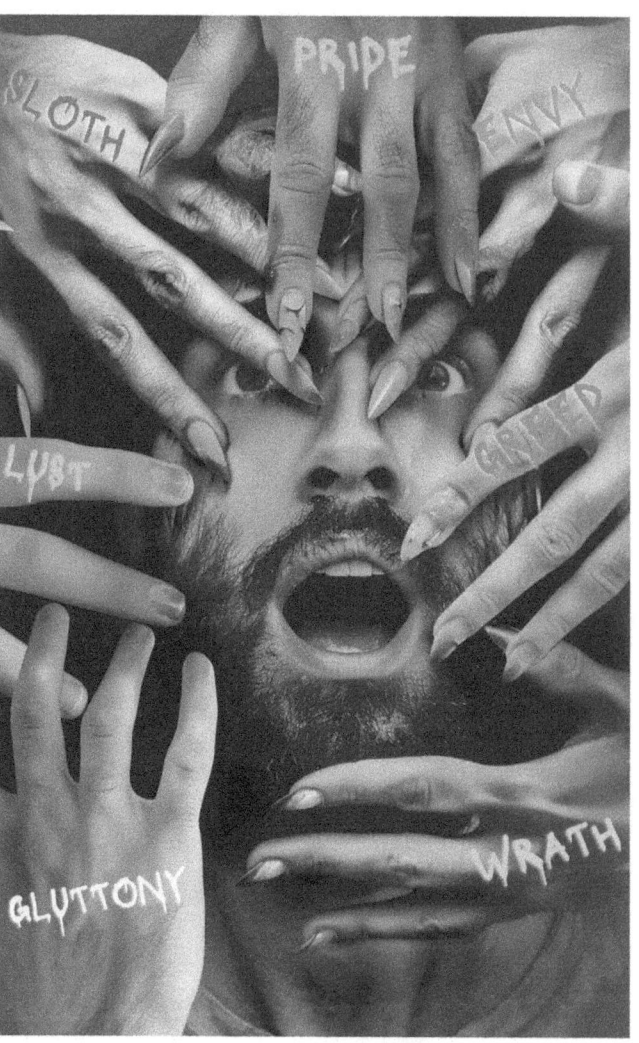

CHAPTER 4

GENERATIONS BECOMING MORE WICKED

In the last chapter, I mentioned Matthew 12:43–45 and how the passage relates to the working of Satan. Let's look at these three verses now.

"When the unclean spirit goes out of a man, he goes through dry places, seeking rest, and finds none. Then he says, 'I will return to my house from which I came.' And when he comes, he finds it empty, swept, and put in order. Then he goes and takes with him seven other spirits more wicked than himself, and they enter and dwell there; and the last state of that man is worse than the first. So shall it also be with this wicked generation" (NKJV).

One thing we see in these verses is that Satan claims that your house is his house and that he can come back and claim the next generation to be even more wicked.

The unclean spirit believes that your house, your seed, your babies, and your children are subjects of his kingdom.

The unclean spirit gets this idea from the chief fallen angel, Satan. Satan claims and believes your children belong to him! Yet, when you came to Christ, He cleaned up your life. The unclean spirit doesn't like that because he has occupied your parents' and grandparents' homes for generations and now he has to leave. But he leaves only for a short time and comes back with seven more evil soldier boys. These unclean spirits don't like being kicked out of the house over which they've had dominion. They want dominion over that family so they can destroy the next generations, so they go after the children.

> **WHO DOES THE DEVIL THINK HE IS TO THINK MY CHILDREN ARE HIS CHILDREN OR THAT MY HOUSE IS HIS HOUSE?**

This pattern of control has been going on for centuries now, and all heaven is upset at this deception. If heaven is upset, then so am I. Who does the devil think he is to think my children are his children or that my house is his house? You see, my house doesn't belong to the devil. My house and my family belong to God. As for me and my house, we will serve the Lord. I am expecting my children, grandchildren, and great-grandchildren to be victorious over family curses. I am claiming the blood of Christ to cover them and to give each generation a true and pure testimony.

"For this purpose the Son of God was manifested, that he might destroy the works of the devil" (1 John 3:8).

"But if we walk in the light, as he is in the light, … the blood of Jesus Christ his Son cleanseth us from all sin" (1 John 1:7).

The Holy Ghost has come in and remodeled your house, and the unclean spirits don't like that. So they come back to move everything back the way things were before the Holy Ghost started playing butler and maid. The Holy Ghost is an interior decorator. When the heavenly Interior Decorator is active in the home, what does Satan frequently do then?

"… seven other spirits more wicked than himself, and they enter in and dwell there; and the last state of the man is worse than the first. Even so shall it be also unto this wicked generation" (Matt. 12:45).

Matthew is talking about generations of families. The devil will come in and attack your children with old familiar sins and old continuous weaknesses—the ones you have had or your father had or even your grandfather or great-grandfather had. The same can also be true from your mother's side of the family. Satan has great advantages. He possesses the wonderful intellectual power of an angel. He was created with the intellectual ability to plan from one generation to the next. He is conscious of his abilities or he could not have instigated a conflict with the mighty God.

"Satan closely watches events … During his experience of nearly six thousand years he has lost none of his skill and shrewdness. All this time he has been a close observer of all that concerns our race" (*Testimonies for the Church*, vol. 2, pp. 171, 172).

"Men and women who have corrupted their own bodies by dissolute habits have also debased their intellects, and destroyed the fine sensibilities of the soul. Very many of this class have married, and left, for an inheritance to their offspring, the taints of their own physical debility and depraved morals. The gratification of animal passions, and gross sensuality, have been the marked characteristics of their posterity, descending from generation to generation, increasing human misery to a fearful degree, and hastening the deprecation of the race" (RH, July 4, 1899, Art. B).

Sin Is at Its Highest Peak

This generation is worse than previous generations because evil spirits have come to fight and attack seven times stronger. Whenever the Holy Ghost does some interior decorating, the evil spirits come after your kids to make them seven times worse.

However, as long as you are in Christ, seeking the Holy Ghost's cleansing, your house does not belong to the devil. Don't let him have any access to your children, your grandchildren, or even your great-grandchildren. Didn't Jesus say that He came to set the captive free? Then our houses belong to the Lord of lords!

Why then is this world becoming so wicked? I believe it is partly due to past generations. Our homes are lacking a cleansing by the Holy Ghost. But there is hope! There is an answer! Don't give up, thinking your generation is totally lost. We will look at some families in the Bible who never gave up, and, as a result, each later generation served the Lord.

Even though God does not put curses on people, people are part of families. Has God left us helpless before the devil's ways and the curse of the law? Absolutely not! When we acknowledge our nature is sinful and confess Jesus as Lord and Savior, we receive a brand new nature, which is the nature of God, and we become new creatures in Christ Jesus, adopted into the family of God where the evil one no longer has a right to us. As a result, we have the rights and dominion of God's kingdom which enable us to exercise authority over all the curses to which the devil has had rights.

We can cut the curse off right now, stopping it from causing any sins to continue in future generations.

"Those from among you shall build the old waste places; you shall raise up the foundations of many generations; and you shall be called the Repairer of the Breach, the Restorer of Streets to Dwell in" (Isa. 58:12, NKJV).

The Hebrew word for "home," or "house," is translated with the understanding of "lines" and "descendants." When you except God's free gift, eternal life, you have a new nature. You have Christ's character implanted within. But what about your descendants, your children? They can receive your weaknesses. Your children must stay in Christ and walk in His Spirit or those weaknesses can become seven times worse. The curse has to be broken with them as well, or the generational sins will continue. How does Satan keep it going? He keeps a precise eye for those new generations so he can attack them too. He goes around like a roaring lion, watching for weaknesses from conception.

The Old Testament talks about spirits that have become "familiar":

"Regard not them that have familiar spirits" (Lev. 19:31).

"And the soul that turns after such as have familiar spirits" (Lev. 20:6).

CHAPTER 5

PARENTS INFLUENCE THE NEXT GENERATION

"As parents you are in a great measure accountable for the souls of your children. You have brought them into existence; and you should, by precept and example, lead them to the Lord and to the courts of heaven. You should impress them with the thought that their temporal interests are of little consequence when compared with their eternal welfare" (*Testimonies for the Church*, vol. 4, p. 113).

As I look at different families over the years of pastoral counseling and pastoral ministry, I see the sins of each father and realize things are being passed on from one generation to the next. There are patterns of families passing down bitterness, heart disease, child abuse, eating disorders, alcoholism, low self-esteem, adultery, and even murder. All of these patterns in our families are really family curses.

"Most assuredly, I say to you, he who believes in Me, the works that I do he will do also; and greater works than these he will do, because I go to My Father" (John 14:12, NKJV).

We must bring Christ into our homes and set the captives free! Generations can be set free by just one person turning to God and staying with God. When people quit praying and reading the Scriptures and when they fellowship with the wrong crowd, stop attending church, or lose their testimony, they will allow curses to come into their homes.

Let's look at a biblical story of the king who ruled in Judaea. Do you remember the story of the three wise men who came to Judaea to talk to the king? They wanted to worship the King of the Jews after following a star they first saw in the east.

"Jesus was born in Bethlehem of Judaea in the days of Herod the king ... When Herod the king had heard these things, he was troubled, and all Jerusalem with him" (Matt. 2:1, 3).

King Herod was troubled about his job security. How could his family rule for generations to come if a king was being born who would have a greater kingdom? The king of the Jews wanted all his descendants to be mighty

Parents Influence the Next Generation

in his kingdom. Herod wanted his children to rule his great kingdom for years to come.

God sent these wise men with the word about the angelic star in the east and about a king to be born. God was offering King Herod a way out of his sinfulness. God sent His word through these wise men, and the king chose not to follow the light he was given. So he went to his counselors and just about anyone else who would listen. He wanted to know if this could be true, about a king being born. These counselors of Herod confirmed that the Scriptures did indeed prophesy about a star from the east and a child king to be the anointed one.

> REMEMBER, THE WORD OF GOD BRINGS LIGHT, AND, IF IT IS REJECTED, THE DARKNESS WILL GET DARKER WITH EACH SUCCEEDING GENERATION.

God was trying to get the king's attention to stop what might be passed on to his children. God sent a supernatural sign and His own word, yet the king rejected them. Remember, the Word of God brings light, and, if it is rejected, the darkness will get darker with each succeeding generation.

Herod the Great came from the generational line of the Edomites, who, for generations, did not heed the Word of God. The Edomites were the cursed children of

Esau. The king had allowed generation after generation of inherited curses and sin to continue on. As the king rejected his chance at freedom from the curse, he became a mass murderer of every male child in His kingdom who were two years old and younger.

Could the king's children also become murderers? Could they even succeed in killing the male child their father was trying to destroy? Or would it take the grandchildren to succeed as murderers?

Herod's Cursed Son and Grandsons

Herod the Great had a son named Herod Antipas. He was born with his father's sins and curses upon him, probably from conception. Mark's Gospel tells us that God wanted to break the curse with Herod Antipas (Mark 6). Herod was very upset that John the Baptist was preaching against sin and adultery—his own personal sin and adultery. Herod Antipas had married the wife of one of his brothers—Herodias was her name. If you remember, Herodias was very upset with John the Baptist and told Herod, "I want him jailed." So Herod had John put in jail.

However, Herod Antipas had some respect for John.

"Herod feared John and protected him, knowing him to be a righteous and holy man. When Herod heard John, he was greatly puzzled; yet he liked to listen to him" (Mark 6:20, NIV).

John the Baptist was a messenger to Herod Antipas as a way to break the generational curse of the Herods. Herod was really being drawn to John's message—the message of God's Word that would bring Herod light and blessings. You probably know the rest of the story. Herod didn't listen, and the curse continued to the next generation.

Then, one evening, Herodias threw a big birthday party for Herod Antipas. All the guests were drunk, and their inhibitions were dulled. The king was perversely inspired by his wife's daughter, Salome, who danced seductively for his party, to grant her one request—even to half of his kingdom. She ran to her mother to decide what to ask, and her mother told her to ask for the head of John the Baptist.

The king knew that, if he refused this request, he would lose his credibility. A king must fulfill his promises. The king could have saved John, but then he would have lost his position and power. Just like his father, he wanted his status to increase. And just like his father, he was cruel and violent, a murderer, repeating his father's curse and sins.

A few years later, Luke tells us that, when Jesus was brought to the king, Herod thought that John the Baptist had been raised from the dead. But he refused to receive Jesus, and the curse continued (Luke 23:8–11; 9:7).

Herod Antipas had a son who carried the name "Herod Agrippa." This son was recorded as hating the church and issuing death decrees against the leaders of Christ's followers.

"And he killed James the brother of John with the sword. And because he saw it pleased the Jews, he proceeded further to take Peter also. ... And when he had apprehended him, he put him in prison ... Peter therefore was kept in prison: but prayer was made without ceasing of the church unto God for him" (Acts 12:2–5).

This Herod continued to be violent, cruel, and murderous. When the angel released Peter, this Herod was so violent and cruel that he had the guards murdered. When God sent an angel to deliver Peter, it was done by a miracle to see if the king would repent to an awesome God. God always gives chance after chance to break your family curses.

We now look at the fourth generation from Herod the Great. There was another Herod Agrippa, and his story is found in the book of Acts, chapters 25 and 26. This story takes place in a courtroom where God had placed the apostle Paul to bring the word of the Lord to this king. God, in His mercy, was still trying to stop the Herod family curse. But even this Herod was too comfortable in his job to give up his big paycheck and turn to God. This Herod wrung out the heart-wrenching words, "Paul, you almost persuade me."

God tried to break the curse with each generation. He came with miracles, supernatural blessings, the spoken word, and each of the Herods rejected Him. They allowed their family curse and sin to intensify and finally wipe out all the Herods.

Satan wants to do the same to your family heritage, but God has given us the gift of His Son as a way of ending all curses. Don't reject this sacrifice!

"Unto Adam also to his wife did the LORD God make coats of skins, and clothed them" (Gen. 3:21).

"Christ hath redeemed us from the curse of the law, being made a curse for us; for it is written, Cursed is every one that hangeth on a tree" (Gal. 3:13).

As parents, we must realize that even in such areas as money we can bring curses upon our children. Are you obsessed with buying? Do you think that if you were in control of money it would give you something? I've realized that the parents who have problems with impulse buying produce children who can't get enough money or material things. Over-spenders create pressure in the home. When pressure builds, we will usually turn to threats, drugs, work, anger, sex, tears, food, persuasion, seduction, logic or anything else to get away from the pressure of impulse buying.

If it's anger in the parents, it's anger that their children will pick up. If it's alcohol or drugs the parents use, it's a drug that the children will usually pick up. Children copy what they see and hear.

I now see that, in my childhood days, it was work, sex, food, and sometimes God that my parents turned to when there was any pressure in the home. I have a work-orientated sibling and a sibling whose life was orientated toward work and sex. I myself have had to turn to God continually for strength from food and sex to handle the pressures of life. I want you to look at what wisdom and knowledge from the past can do for me now. I see how Satan attacked my family, and now I can walk in God's light.

"For you were sometimes darkness, but now are ye light in the Lord: walk as children of light" (Eph. 5:8).

The Word of God warns us all not to turn to the ways which we have learned or have been taught. If we have accepted Jesus Christ, He will enable us to start a new lifestyle.

"But without faith it is impossible to please Him, for he who comes to God must believe that He is, and that He is a rewarder of those who diligently seek Him" (Heb. 11:6, NKJV).

Our children will be changed as they see their parents turn to the Lord. The Bible says that, if we raise up our children in the ways of the Lord, when they are old, they will not depart from our instruction (Prov. 22:6).

CHAPTER 6

THE FAMILY WAS BLESSED

When Christ the Son created the original family, His blessings were with Him. Adam and Eve, along with their children, had dominion over all living things. But, as soon as sin entered the garden, curses were allowed on God's creations.

When Adam and Eve sinned, they saw their nakedness and hid themselves. The Hebrew understanding of "nakedness" is more in line with Genesis 3, which illustrates that they saw themselves as capable of being crafty, or subtle, like the serpent.

Another way of bringing curses is by hiding ourselves. When we try to work our way out of sinful situations, we can pass on that curse to our children. Adam and Eve try to run and hide from their sin problem. As soon as they sinned, God brought a way out of the sin. But the first family tried to hide behind their good works and satisfy

God. It is only through the shedding of blood that sin could be forgiven. "Unto Adam also and to his wife did the LORD God make coats of skin, and clothed them" (Gen. 3:21, NKJV). Could the sin of "righteousness by works" still be passed down to the first generation of children?

Genesis 4:1, 2 says: "And Adam knew Eve his wife; and she conceived, and bare Cain, and said, I have gotten a man from the LORD. And she again bare his brother Abel. And Abel was a keeper of the sheep, but Cain was a tiller of the ground." I used to think that God cursed Adam and his family, but as I read the first family's sinful story, I saw that only the serpent and the ground were verbally cursed by God (Gen. 3:14–18). When Adam and Eve had true repentance and allowed God to place coats of skin upon them, they escaped any curse. They had found that God's mercy and forgiveness came only through the shedding of blood.

During a process of time it came to pass that Cain and his brother Abel were to bring an offering unto the Lord (Gen. 4:3). God accepted Abel's offering but had no respect for Cain's offering. The parents of these two young men almost hid behind their own righteousness and brought a curse to themselves. They did indeed allow for the serpent to have access to tempt their children to become self-righteous. For a short time, Adam and Eve felt that they had no need for Christ's righteousness. But they finally allowed him to put coats of skin upon them, accepting Christ's work instead of their own works of the leaf coverings.

"Cain thought him righteous, and he came to God with a thank offering only. He made no confession of sin, and acknowledged no need of mercy. But Abel came with the blood that pointed to the Lamb of God. He came as a sinner, confessing himself lost; his only hope was the unmerited love of God" (*Christ's Object Lessons*, p. 152).

> **GOD GAVE THE FIRST FAMILY THE BLESSING OF DOMINION, AND THE SAME GOD RESTORES DOMINION TO THE HUMAN FAMILY.**

"Blessed are the poor in spirit; for theirs is the kingdom of heaven" (Matt. 5:3).

God gave the first family the blessing of dominion, and the same God restores dominion to the human family. It is the blood of Christ that restores a family to be blessed for generations. Without a blood sacrifice, Cain and his descendants brought curses to the human race. Cain's evil works—righteousness by works—led him to fall short of the blood of Christ, and righteousness by works are proving the ruins of thousands today.

God Blesses Abraham and Esau Brings a Curse

In the 13th chapter of Genesis, God promises to bless Abraham's seed. God is always ready to give blessings instead of curses. When Isaac was grown and enjoying God's blessing, Abraham's seed was full of blessings. Scripture also tells about how Jacob was a blessing to the family. Scripture also reveals that Esau wanted to disobey and manipulate his father.

You probably think Esau blew it by selling his birthright. But what really bothered Esau's family the most was his treating the things of God lightly. He was somewhat sorry about the situation of selling his birthright, but he never repented of his sin. He just developed a vengeful, manipulating attitude.

"And Esau was forty years old when he took to wife Judith the daughter of Beeri the Hittite, and Bashemath the daughter of Elon the Hittite: which were a grief of mind unto Isaac and to Rebekah" (Gen. 26:34).

Esau did indeed sell his birthright, and his actions brought failure and continued curse upon himself.

"But there's something else Esau did. He married Hittites. Esau had two Hittite wives. Isaac and Rebekah were very grieved over Esau's marrying those two women. They had sent Jacob up to Laban to get a wife, but what was the problem with Esau getting Hittite wives?

The Hittites descended from Noah's disrespectful son, Ham, through his son, Canaan. A curse had been placed on Canaan—apparently a generational curse. By marrying Hittite women, Esau was bringing that curse into the family of Isaac. (See https://1ref.us/me02 and Gen. 9:24.)

We can look at Scripture and realize that Esau was bringing curses onto his family (a generational curse). Isaac and Rebekah didn't want Esau marrying just anyone, so they sent Jacob to Laban to arrange a wife for Esau. The problem was that Esau wanted Hittite women, and these women were descendants of Canaan whose descendants were a cursed generation with sexual immorality and pridefulness. When Scripture tells us not to be "unequally yoked," and we follow our pride and do our own way, we bring a curse upon us (2 Cor. 6:14).

Marrying an Unbeliever

You may be wondering—What if I have already married an unbeliever or if I am already unequally yoked? What if I became a born-again believer after marriage and my spouse has not? Well, you can look to Scripture and see that all curses can be broken.

"And if a woman has a husband who is not a believer and he is willing to live with her, she must not divorce him. For the unbelieving husband has been sanctified through his wife, and the unbelieving wife has been sanctified through her believing husband. Otherwise your children would be unclean, but as it is, they are holy" (1 Cor. 7:13, 14, NIV).

Paul is saying that God will save one person in a family, and that person can set others free from prison. Therefore, one believing mate sanctifies the household, and the children are freed from any family curse. The conversion and behavior of a spouse will be the greatest Christian witness any unbelieving spouse will ever notice. If the believing spouse will love the other spouse as Christ loved the church, that love will be irresistible.

"Wives, likewise, be submissive to your own husbands, that even if some do not obey the word, they, without a word, may be won by the conduct of their wives" (1 Peter 3:1, NKJV).

So don't backslide. Stay with God and pray for your spouse. If you turn away from God, the curse will probably return seven times worse. Backsliding costs too much—affecting you and the next generation of your family.

God "had separated Abraham from his idolatrous kindred, that the patriarch might train and educate his family apart from the seductive influences which would have surrounded them in Mesopotamia, and that the true faith might be preserved in its purity by his descendants from generation to generation" (*Patriarchs and Prophets*, pp. 141, 142).

It is in coming to the Lord Jesus Christ that you have begun to break any curse. So, if God says don't be unequally yoked together, don't invite a curse upon yourself and your future. Isaac and Rebekah were very upset about their son marrying a Canaanite and allowing a curse to start in their family.

"Parental indulgence causes disorder [curses] in families and in society. It confirms in the young the desire to follow inclination, instead of submitting to the divine requirements. Thus they grow up with a heart adverse to doing God's will, and they transmit their irreligious, insubordinate spirit to the children and children's children" (ibid., p. 142).

In Exodus you can see that God is concerned about the family of Israel, and He is concerned about all of our families. He wants to pass blessings on from generation to generation. Some of your good traits and strengths have come from previous generations. Your spirituality has come down from your parents, grandparents, or even great grandparents. Someone has been praying for you, and you have received blessings. Obedience to the Word of God, as you continue to grow, will bring blessings upon blessings.

"Thus says the LORD: 'Cursed is the man who trusts in man and makes flesh his strength, whose heart departs from the LORD' " (Jer. 17:5, NKJV).

CHAPTER 7

GETTING OUT FROM FAMILY CURSES

You know the story of Moses, Pharaoh, and the Egyptians. The Israelites were slaves to the Egyptians. God, in His mercy, raised up an Israelite who was an adopted son to the Egyptian king. This adopted son was to be the deliver of God's chosen people from Pharaoh's captivity.

"Then Moses said, 'Thus says the LORD: "About midnight I will go out into the midst of Egypt; and all the firstborn in the land of Egypt shall die, from the firstborn of Pharaoh who sits on his throne, even to the firstborn of the female servant who is behind the handmill, and all the firstborn of the animals. Then there shall be a great cry throughout all the land of Egypt, such as was not like it before, nor shall be like it again" ' " (Exod. 11:4–6, NKJV).

Moses continued to warn Pharaoh, and each time he did, the king refused to listen, and the curse stayed upon Pharaoh and his family and his kingdom. Plagues came. There were frogs, filthy water, bugs, drought, and troubles on the land. Yet, the king continue to reject the mercy of God, and the curses continued upon Pharaoh.

Even though the Egyptians were not enslaved as the Israelites were, they, nonetheless, were under Pharaoh's curse. God stated that He was going to judge the Egyptian family, taking the firstborn of each Egyptian family. Why? Because they were under the king's curse. Why were they under the king's curse? The Egyptians were also into sin. They started worshiping Pharaoh's idols and giving into sinful ways. God gave the Egyptians miracle after miracle, but they would not repent.

God is very concerned that generational curses be stopped. That is why He was willing to completely wipe out the Herods, the Canaanites, and Pharaoh's clan.

"And Ezra blessed the LORD, the great God. And all the people answered, Amen, Amen, with lifting up their hands: and they bowed their heads, and worshipped the LORD with their faces to the ground" (Neh. 8:6).

"Yet even here was evidence of the sin of Israel. Through the intermarriage of the people with other nations, the Hebrew language had become corrupted, and great care was necessary on the part of the speakers to explain the law in the language of the people, that it might be understood by all" (*Prophets and Kings*, pp. 661, 662).

When God's people intermarry with non-believers, it is hard for the children to see the complete consecrated way. For this reason, in many instances in Scripture, God had to wipe out children as well. This would cause the curses to stop among God's people.

Joshua tells about the life of Achan in the book of Joshua, chapter 7.

"And Joshua, and all Israel with him, took Achan the son of Zerah, and the silver, and the garment, and the wedge of gold, and his sons and his daughters … And all Israel stoned him with stones, and burned them with fire, after they had stoned them with stones" (Joshua 7:24, 25).

This father was from the tribe of Judah. He was a son of royal heritage and a fellow believer. But Achan stole a Babylonian garment and some gold and silver. Achan never repented and therefore never sanctified his family. (Israel saw the curse of Achan's family, and God allowed his wife and children to be stoned and burned.) God does not want the next generation to be cursed. So Achan paid a heavy price for not repenting.

When one believer repents, it can restore the whole household—especially if it is the priest of the home. "The house of the righteous shall stand" (Prov. 12:7). "Through wisdom is an house built" (Prov. 24:3).

Through intermarriage, a friendship had been brought about between Eliashib the high priest and Tobiah the Ammonite, Israel's bitter enemy. As a result of this unhallowed alliance, Eliashib had allowed Tobiah to occupy an apartment connected with the temple, which in previous times was used as a storeroom for tithes and offerings given by the people.

> **WHEN GOD'S PEOPLE MARRY UNBELIEVERS, GENERATIONS DOWN CAN BE DEEPLY AND FOREVER CURSED.**

When God's people marry unbelievers, generations down can be deeply and forever cursed.

"Because of the cruelty and treachery of the Ammonites and Moabites toward Israel, God had declared through Moses that they should be forever shut out from the congregation of His people. See Deuteronomy 23:3–6. In defiance of this word, the high priest had cast out the offerings stored in the chambers of God's house, to make a place for this representative of a proscribed race" (*Prophets and Kings*, pp. 669, 670).

"Not only had the temple been profaned, but the offerings had been misapplied. This had tended to discourage the liberalities of the people. They had lost their zeal and fervor, and were reluctant to pay their tithes. The treasuries of the Lord's house were poorly

Getting Out from Family Curses

supplied; many of the singers and others employed in the temple service, not receiving sufficient support, had left the work of God to labor elsewhere" (ibid., p. 670).

When God's people don't obey His word, curses will ensue. During the time of Nehemiah, God's church suffered financially. It took Nehemiah several generations to restore God's treasury.

"Thus saith the Lord, cursed be the man that trusteth in man, and maketh flesh his arm, and whose heart departeth from the Lord" (Jer. 17:5).

Eliashib, the high priest, put trust in Tobiah the Ammonite, and God's temple and people suffered a curse. We see this in our churches and our political systems today. We tend to rely on someone's good looks, intellectual ability, or charisma. We shouldn't put our trust in someone's ability or good looks or any other human trait. We need to only put our trust in God the Father. Otherwise, we will be bringing a curse upon our church and our nation.

We see couples getting married, and they do the drop-out thing with God and His people. They want a husband or wife so bad. Then they give up the Lord. They're putting their trust in a human and bringing a curse on their marriage. "And whatsoever ye do [including marriage], do it heartily, as to the Lord, and not unto men" (Col. 3:23). Intermarriage with the heathen does cost you. Many people steal from God by putting trust in their work or possessions. You may say, "I can't afford to tithe," but you mean, "I trust my job and money more than I trust God's Word." Malachi 3:9, NKJV, says, "You are cursed with a curse, for you have robbed Me."

"Another result of intercourse with idolaters was a disregard of the Sabbath, the sign distinguishing the Israelites from all other nations as worshipers of the true God" (*Patriarchs and Prophets*, p. 671).

"Their religion continued to be a mixture of Judaism and heathenism, and their claim to be the people of God was the source of schism, emulation, and enmity between the two nations, from generation to generation" (*Prophets and Kings*, pp. 674, 675).

Just like the family of Pharaoh or like the family of Moses, we as parents can have an everlasting effect for our generation and for generations to come.

"Those who are contemplating marriage should consider what will be the character and influence of the home they are founding. As they become parents, a sacred trust is committed to them. Upon them depends in a great measure the well-being of their children in this world, and their happiness in the world to come" (*The Ministry of Healing*, p. 357).

One believing person in a household, through prayer and the Word of God, can sanctify the household and free your children from any generational curse (1 Cor.

7:13, 14; 1 Peter 3:1, 2). Staying with Christ can put the blood on your doorposts and cover the whole family.

CHAPTER 8

BLOOD REVERSES ALL CURSES

When I damaged my spiritual life by becoming a bartender, I felt as if there wasn't any way out. But as my mother and others continued to pray the Word of God over me, the Spirit of God pricked my heart. Two thoughts came to my mind: "And they overcame by the blood of the Lamb," and "Redeemed how I love to proclaim it. Redeemed by the blood of the Lamb." It was the word "blood" that caught my ears and brought me out of a family curse.

When Job repented, God said, "Offer a sacrifice" and "pray for those friends of yours."

"Therefore take unto you now seven bullocks and seven rams, and go to my servant Job, and offer up for yourselves a burnt offering; and my servant Job shall pray for you ... And the LORD turned the captivity of Job, when he prayed for his friends: also the LORD gave Job twice as much as he had before" (Job 42:8, 10).

I started praying for those whom I had led astray and for those who led me astray. When we do this, we will be at the beginning of deliverance. "Love your enemies, bless them that curse you, do good to them that hate you, and pray for them which despitefully use you, and persecute you" (Matt. 5:44).

I was afraid of not being accepted, so I fell to the world of bartending and the night life. I wanted so much to be accepted by the men in my life (my dad, my brothers, and others). The fear of not being accepted led me into a curse. I enjoy male company looking up to me, talking to me, listening to me, and just plain accepting me. Most of my customers were men. Very few women stayed long or returned each and every night like the men did.

"For the thing which I greatly feared is come upon me, and that which I was afraid of is come unto me" (Job 3:25). "All my bones shook" (Job 4:14, GW).

It seems that my weakness was already known to the evil one because he was able to exploit my weakness so thoroughly. Was it also Job's own fearfulness that contributed to the curse that Satan put upon him?

Two Cherubs and Two Angels

God always makes a way to break a sin. When our first parents sinned, God quickly showed how to reverse that sin and stop the curse.

"Unto Adam also and to his wife did the Lord God make coats of skins, and clothed them" (Gen. 3:21).

"God was the first to kill and the first to shed blood. He shed blood to show that blood was the solution to the curse of sin. When Cain and Abel were born to our first parents, they knew full well that Mom and Dad had sinned and that God's shedding of blood was their only way to deliverance. Cain ignored the blood and instead brought the vegetables which he grew. Abel brought a lamb from his flock because he knew that blood would break the curse. Cain chose to ignore that there could be a curse for sin, just as there are people today who choose to ignore that sin can bring a curse" (Marilyn Hickey, *Breaking Generational Curses*, p. 31).

When Adam and Eve were cast out of the garden, the Lord sent a flaming sword to guard the entrance. On either side was a cherub. This was a foreshadowing of the death and resurrection of Jesus. Jesus' death and resurrection were an act of God's mercy and justice.

The sword that blocked Eden's gate was the symbol of the Word. For "The Word of God cuts like a two-edged sword." "The Word of God never fails." "We must eat the Word." "Christ abides in His followers through the Word." "The Word is bread from heaven." May I suggest that the sword is the Word of God, and John tells us that the Word of God became flesh (John 1:14). Therefore, the garden account was pointing to Jesus and His free mercy. Years later, Moses provided the first physical mercy seat. In Exodus 25 and 26, God instructed His leader how to make the tabernacle.

"Make an atonement cover of pure gold—two and a half cubits long and a cubit and a half wide. And make two cherubim out of hammered gold at the ends of the cover. Make one cherub on one end and the second cherub on the other; make the cherubim of one piece with the cover, at the two ends. The cherubim are to have their wings spread upward, overshadowing the cover with them. The cherubim are to face each other, looking toward the cover. Place the cover on top of the ark and put in the ark the tablets of the covenant law that I will give you. There, above the cover between the two cherubim that are over the ark of the covenant law, I will meet with you and give you all my commands for the Israelites" (Exod. 25:17–22, NIV).

This was to show that God didn't judge your sins but that they were judged through a blood offering. This blood offering will break any generational curse. God's mercy and justice are forever satisfied by this sacrifice.

Now let's look at the Gospels' account of Jesus' death. The followers of Jesus looked into His tomb and saw two figures, one at the head where His body lay and one at the feet. These two figures were dressed in white just as the two cherubs at Eden's gate were dressed as they held their flaming swords, which represented Jesus as our mercy seat. Jesus' freely shed blood breaks sin's curse. Truly, all mercy and justice is satisfied because of the ultimate sacrifice—the blood of Jesus.

> **JESUS' FREELY SHED BLOOD BREAKS SIN'S CURSE. TRULY, ALL MERCY AND JUSTICE IS SATISFIED BECAUSE OF THE ULTIMATE SACRIFICE—THE BLOOD OF JESUS.**

Moses stood between two hills giving blessings and curses. Could this be a foreshadowing to God's people of mercy on one side and justice on the other? Choose today God's blood and be set free. Sampson cried out between two pillars and received God's mercy and justice, and he was found accepted.

On Mount Calvary, Jesus hung between two other trees, each bearing a thief. One thief cried for Jesus' mercy and got justice too. The other cried for nothing, but relied on himself, and received only justice without mercy.

It was at the cross that God the Father gave us the true mercy seat. All who come under His Son's blood are already judged.

"Children of the Lord, how precious is the promise! How full the atonement of the Saviour for our guilt! The Redeemer, with a heart of unalterable love, still pleads His sacred blood in the sinner's behalf. The wounded hands, the pierced side, the marred feet, plead eloquently for fallen man, whose redemption is purchased at such an infinite cost. Oh, matchless condescension! Neither time nor events can lessen the efficacy of the atoning sacrifice. As the fragrant cloud of incense rose acceptably to heaven, and Aaron sprinkled the blood upon the mercy seat of ancient Israel and cleansed the people from guilt, so the merits of the slain Lamb are accepted by God today as a purifier from defilement of sin" (*Testimonies for the Church*, vol. 4, p. 124).

What Communion Wine Symbolizes

Our Lord has said, "Unless ye eat the flesh of the Son of Man and drink His blood, you have no life in you ... For My flesh is food indeed, and my blood is drink indeed" (John 6:53, 55, NKJV).

"How little children are educated to study the Bible as the word of God, and feed upon its truths, which are the flesh and blood of the Son of God! ... Whoso eateth My flesh, and drinketh My blood [that is, continues to receive the words of Christ and practices them], hath eternal life" (*Fundamentals of Christian Education*, p. 386).

The communion service should point to Christ's second coming. It was designed to keep this hope vivid in the disciples' minds as well as in ours. Remember always that the communion service is not to be a season of sadness or an occasion to shy away from. It is a service that gives hope to a cursed generation.

"It is only because of His death that we can look with joy to His second coming. His sacrifice is the center of our hope. Upon this we must fix our faith" (*The Desire of Ages*, p. 660).

Sin brings a curse. Blood brings a blessed hope. Stay with Christ, and He will draw your family unto a "thousand generations" (Deut. 7:9).

CHAPTER 9

BREAKING THE FAMILY CURSE OF NOAH

As I was reading from the book, *Breaking Generational Curses*, I was amazed at the author's view of Noah's family curse. So I did my own study. It was very interesting. Let's take a look at the biblical account of Noah in Genesis, chapter 9.

"And Noah began to be a farmer, and he planted a vineyard. Then he drank of the wine and was drunk, and became uncovered in his tent. And Ham, the father of Canaan, saw the nakedness of his father, and told his two brothers outside. But Shem and Japheth took a garment, laid it on both their shoulders, and went backward and covered the nakedness of their father. Their faces were turned away, and they did not see their father's nakedness. So Noah awoke from his wine, and knew what his younger son had done to him. Then he said: 'Cursed be Canaan; A servant of servants He shall be to his brethren.' And he said: 'Blessed be the LORD, The God of Shem, And may Canaan be his servant. May God enlarge Japheth, And may he dwell in the tents of Shem; And may Canaan be his servant.' And Noah lived after the flood three hundred and fifty years. So all the days of Noah were nine hundred and fifty years; and he died" (Gen. 9:20–29, NKJV).

Here is definitely the beginning of a family curse or the start of generational sins. In Proverbs 26:2, God tells us that there is a cause for any curse. The devil's favorite avenue for any curse is through the mind.

"Satan is ever seeking to impress and control the mind, and none of us are safe except as we have a constant connection with God" (*Testimonies for the Church*, vol. 4, p. 542).

"Satan's influence is constantly exerted upon men to distract the senses, control the mind for evil, and incite to violence and crime" (*The Desire of Ages*, p. 341).

Noah got drunk. Alcohol is a tool for sin. Satan will use it to bring a terrible curse upon the family. Noah should have never found himself in this situation. But when people get drunk (even a little lightheaded), they do things they regret because their will is broken down. Noah was abused, probably sexually. That is why the Bible mentions his being "uncovered" and Ellen White describes his crime as "unnatural." Could this be earth's first homosexual beginnings? That's what "uncovered" means in the old Hebrew language. "The unnatural crime of Ham declared that filial reverence had long before been cast from his soul, and it revealed the impiety and vileness of his character" (*Patriarchs and Prophets*, p. 117).

The book of Habakkuk links strong drink and a sexual situation.

"Woe to him who gives drink to his neighbor, Pressing him to your bottle, Even to make him drunk, That you may look on his nakedness! You are filled with shame instead of glory. You also—drink! And be exposed as uncircumcised! The cup of the LORD's right hand will be turned against you, And utter shame will be on your glory" (Hab. 2:15, 16, NKJV).

Isn't this what happened to Noah? Isn't this what's happening to our teens and our adulterous adults? Noah, speaking by divine inspiration, foretold the history of Ham's descendants by putting the curse on his grandson Canaan. Studies show that children who are sexually abused or who are in sexually perverted homes are usually abusive too or they continue sexual perversions into their adult lives. Canaan may have been sexually abused or he may have seen so much of his father's perversion that he could not but be consumed. "All should guard the senses, lest Satan gain victory over them, for these are the avenues of the soul" (*The Adventist Home*, p. 401).

Noah's son Ham had four sons—Canaan, Mizraim, Cush, and Phut. Noah's grandson Canaan was cursed.

"You shall not bow down to them nor serve them. For I, the LORD your God, am a jealous God, visiting the iniquity of the fathers upon the children to the third and fourth generations of those who hate Me" (Exod. 20:5, NKJV).

If you follow Ham's curse down the generations, you see how it started with Ham and continued down the next three generations just as God said it would. When a father commits a sin, his son picks it up. There is a breakdown or weakness already to sin, and the old nature, which comes from the father, is passed onto the son. Then the devil comes in to attack the son seven times stronger, and he falls into it too.

God destroyed Gomorrah for many reasons but especially for sexual perversion. He also had to destroy Sodom for its sin of homosexuality. Sodom and Gomorrah were directly descended from Canaan. You can follow the Canaanites all the way down to the time of Joshua. They were into total sexual pleasures, including sexual activity in front of idols. As generations of sin go on, the sin gets worse in each later generation. The more people sin, the better Satan makes them at it.

Billy Graham once said, "If God doesn't come soon, He will have to apologize to Sodom and Gomorrah." There are curses that come down and attack a generation, and they have to be broken for them not to continue. You must break the curse on your family. By so doing, you can break Satan's power over you and your family.

Do you know what provoked the curse in Noah's family? His own drunkenness. Grandpa Noah got drunk, and that indiscretion opened the way for sin. Why do you believe drinking is such a little thing? Proverbs 20:1, NKJV, says: "Wine is a mocker, strong drink is a brawler, and whoever is led astray by it is not wise." In her book, *Breaking Generational Curses*, Marilyn Hickey makes the point that because leaders might be called at any time to handle an emergency—and their actions at such a time affect a multitude of people--a leader should not drink *ever*.

> **GRANDPA NOAH GOT DRUNK, AND THAT INDISCRETION OPENED THE WAY FOR SIN.**

"Must the curse of intemperance forever rest like a blight upon the civilized world? Must it continue to sweep, every year, like a devouring fire over over thousands of happy homes?" (*The Ministry of Healing*, p. 344).

We continue to see the curse of this evil substance. It would do well if you would follow the instructions of Proverbs 23:20, NKJV: "Do not mix with winebibbers, or with gluttonous eaters of meat." Isaiah says, "Woe to those who rise early in the morning, that they may follow intoxicating drink; who continue until night, till wine inflames them!" (Isa. 5:11, NKJV).

Why does the Bible warn about strong drink? What will happen if you continue to drink? Not only will it destroy you, but you will have placed a curse upon your family and your descendants.

"Our only safety is in rejecting firmly the first approach to presumption. God has, through the merits of Christ, given us sufficient grace to withstand Satan and be more than conquerors. Resistance is success. 'Resist the devil, and he will flee from you.' James 4:7. Resistance must be firm and steadfast. We lose all we gain if we resist today only to yield tomorrow" (*Testimonies for the Church*, vol. 3, p. 482).

Chapter 10

FAMILY TRADITIONS OR GENERATIONAL CURSES?

I once heard the song "Family Tradition" on a country western station. In it, Hank Williams, Jr., gives "family tradition" as the reason he smokes, drinks, gets stoned, and carouses.

This song has more truth in it if looked at it through biblical eyes! Satan is truly causing generation after generation to fall into sin. Some call it tradition. The Bible calls it sin.

God has always wanted blessings upon blessings bestowed upon His people—especially upon the family. Let's look at five divine institutions:

1. The first is the freedom of choice, or free will. Genesis, chapter 2, deals with the gift of freedom of choice.

2. The second is marriage—also found in Genesis, chapter 2. God intended for us to marry.
3. The Sabbath as a family blessing—from sundown to sundown—also found in Genesis, chapter 2.
4. The family institution, discussed in Genesis, chapters 3 and 4.
5. God would protect our individual rights through small nations. God never wanted one nation to rule all others.

Didn't God want the family blessed? God put His blessing on Adam and Eve, and He gave them and their children dominion. But they sinned, and sin always brings the curse. When they first sinned, God went quickly to stop the curse, by the shedding of blood. He clothed them with animal skins (Gen. 3:21). Instantly, Adam and Eve saw a way out from their curse, and they had access to God's mercy.

Blood on the Doorposts

God wanted to bless the family of Israel. From the Garden of Eden to Seth's family up to Abraham's family, God wanted to give blessings. As we come to the story of Moses and his Egyptian friends, we see that the blood can save families. We also see that, if there is no blood over a family, that family is usually destroyed.

Family Traditions or Generational Curses?

"Moses, said, 'Thus says the LORD: "About midnight I will go throughout Egypt, and all the firstborn in the land of Egypt will die … There will be a great cry throughout the whole land of Egypt, such as there has never been, nor ever will be again" ' " (Exod. 11:4–6, NET).

That's part of the story of Pharaoh enslaving God's people and God raising up a commandment-keeping man to bring deliverance. Moses warned this ungodly king over and over again, but Pharaoh stopped listening and his people, including all his children, were under a curse. Scripture says—

> **MOSES WARNED THIS UNGODLY KING OVER AND OVER AGAIN, BUT PHARAOH STOPPED LISTENING AND HIS PEOPLE, INCLUDING ALL HIS CHILDREN, WERE UNDER A CURSE.**

"Tell the whole community of Israel that on the tenth day of this month each man is to take a lamb for his family, one for each household. If any household is too small for a whole lamb, they must share one with their nearest neighbor, having taken into account the number of people there are" (Exod. 12:3, 4a, NIV).

God wants every person in the household to be saved. That is why He wants Moses to tell them to take "into account the number of people there are." I believe God also meant for all of the Egyptians and all their families to be saved too. But they heard only the voice of Pharaoh and were let astray. I believe that some of the Egyptians were saved. Scripture goes on to say—

"The animals you choose must be year-old males without defect, and you may take them from the sheep or the goats. Take care of them until the fourteenth day of the month, when all the members of the community of Israel must slaughter them at twilight. Then they are to take some of the blood and put it on the sides and tops of the doorframes of the houses where they eat the lambs" (Exod. 12:5–7, NIV).

"All the firstborn are mine; for on the day that I smote all the firstborn in the land of Egypt I hallowed unto me all the firstborn in Israel, both man and beast: mine shall they be" (Num. 3:13).

"That same night they are to eat the meat roasted over the fire, along with bitter herbs, and bread made without yeast. ... 'On that same night I will pass through Egypt and strike down every firstborn of both men and animals, and I will bring judgment on all the gods of Egypt. I am the LORD. The blood will be a sign for you on the houses where you are, and when I see the blood, I will pass over you. No destructive plague will touch you when I strike Egypt' " (Exod. 12:8, 12, 13, NIV).

What will save you and your family? Only the blood of Jesus. It's not in reading all of Mrs. White's writings or spanking your children. It's not in psychology or

Family Traditions or Generational Curses? 95

ministry. The blood of Jesus alone will save. If you were to die tonight, do you know for sure you are ready? The key to being ready is the blood of Jesus, nothing else. The Israelites understood that the blood was the key to their family. The blood is the key to *your* family.

"We need to show our children the truth—'Hey, if you curse me, and act rebelliously toward me, you're putting a curse on yourself;' or, 'If you get into sexual sins, you're putting a curse on yourself' " (*Breaking Generational Curses*, p. 67).

Tell your children that you've been cleansed of your past and explain anything they ask. Show how God is blessing your family because of your repentance and the blood of Jesus covering you.

CHAPTER 11

BITTERNESS IN PARENTS OR LEADERS—CURSES

"The Saviour's words of reproof to the men of Nazareth applied, in the case of Paul, not only to the unbelieving Jews, but to his own brethren in the faith. Had the leaders in the church fully surrendered their feeling of bitterness toward the apostle, and accepted him as one specially called of God to bear the gospel to the gentiles, the Lord would have spared him to them. God had not ordained that Paul's labors should so soon end, but He did not work a miracle to counteract the train of circumstances to which the course of the leaders in the church at Jerusalem had given rise" (*The Acts of Apostles*, p. 417).

As you see bitterness in your life, remember that it must be turned over to God. A lady once said to me, "I don't ever want to talk about my mother! She is my worst enemy." When I asked her why, she told me she wasn't even able to talk about it. I could see she was very bitter. As I got to know her children, they were also very bitter—towards the church and the church school because they had once been mistreated.

The Bible tells us that many will be defiled, "Looking diligently lest any man fail of the grace of God; lest any root of bitterness springing up trouble you, and thereby many be defiled [cursed]" (Heb. 12:15). Bitterness can truly be a cause of family curses in the home and in the church family. If people who, because of bad situations or because of being mistreated, become bitter and do not forgive, their family and children's future family will miss out on the family blessing.

I believe forgiveness is a kind of obedience that brings reversal to the curse of bitterness. As Christ hung on the cross He did not at any point become bitter toward those who professed to be His followers or even toward any who nailed Him to the cross or had any part in His death.

"I even I, am he that blotteth out thy transgressions for mine own sake, and will not remember thy sins" (Isa. 43:25).

"And when ye stand praying, forgive … But if ye do not forgive, neither will your Father which is in heaven forgive your trespasses" (Mark 11:25, 26).

"Bitterness is a luxury you cannot afford. It's too expensive. It will defile you, and it will defile those around you … That's exactly what happened to Esau. When Esau became bitter against Jacob and Jacob's descendants, his children became bitter against them too" (*Breaking Generational Curses*, p. 86).

If you look at Esau and his descendants, you see that they made things hard for the Israelites, they tried to stop their entrance into the Promise Land (see Num. 20:10-21). Bitterness toward anyone or any group will cause you to lose blessings. Dear reader, has someone hurt you or defiled you in any way? Don't become bitter. Is your husband or wife not meeting all your needs? Don't become bitter! Instead, teach your children to love their enemies and pray for their friends. Teach them that they can bring a curse upon them if they become bitter.

"But I say to you, Love your enemies, bless them that curse you, do good to them that hate you, and pray for them which despitefully use you, and persecute you" (Matt. 5:44).

Job did not want his family to be under a curse. When Job was being attacked, he kept his faith. "If I rejoiced at the destruction of him that hated me, or lifted up myself when evil found him: Neither have I suffered my mouth to sin by wishing a curse to his soul" (Job 31:29, 30).

The Whole Church Suffers

In dealing with erring church members, God's people are to carefully follow the instruction given by the Lord in Matthew 18:15. "If thy brother shall trespass against thee, go and tell him his fault between thee and him alone." When this method is not followed by God's people—especially leaders—that church is cursed, and it could effect even the families of the church.

"One person is told, then another, and still another; and continually the report grows, and the evil increases, till the whole church is made to suffer. Settle the matter 'between thee and him alone.' This is God's plan. 'Go not forth hastily to strive, lest thou know not what to do in the end thereof, when thy neighbor hath put thee to shame. Debate thy cause with thy neighbor himself; and discover not a secret to another' Proverbs 25:8, 9" (*Testimonies for the Church*, vol. 7, p. 260).

Bitterness is used many times in the understanding of hatred or malice in the Scriptures. Whatever the situation, God still expects you to follow the plan that He gave for the settlement of problems or personal injustices.

"Do not suffer resentment to ripen into malice. Do not allow the wound to fester and break out in poisoned words, which taint the minds of those who hear. Do not allow bitter thoughts to continue to fill your mind and his. Go to your brother, and in humility and sincerity talk with him about the matter" (ibid., p. 261).

Many a minister's family has been wounded by the gossip and rumors in God's church. Don't let God's church family bring a curse upon itself with bitterness or malice toward any part of God's family. Do you want to reverse the church's curse? People may dislike you, gossip about you, say terrible things about you. Do what God says and bring blessings to your family and your church.

> **DON'T LET GOD'S CHURCH FAMILY BRING A CURSE UPON ITSELF WITH BITTERNESS OR MALICE TOWARD ANY PART OF GOD'S FAMILY.**

"But I say unto you, Love your enemies, bless them that curse you, do good to them that hate you, and pray for them which despitefully use you, and persecute you" (Matt. 5:44).

"Therefore if thine enemy hunger, feed him; if he thirst, give him drink: for in so doing thou shalt heap coals of fire on his head. Be not overcome of evil, but overcome evil with good" (Rom. 12:20, 21).

If you will follow God's way, people will become silent or thank you for your concern and become part of your support.

"When a man's ways please the LORD, he maketh even his enemies to be at peace with him" (Prov. 16:7).

"To the hungry soul every bitter thing is sweet" (Prov. 27:7).

"Husbands, love your wives, and be not bitter against them" (Col. 3:19).

When you are hurting the worst, go to your secret prayer closet and weep out all your bitterness. Jesus wept. Peter wept bitterly! Peter carried with him the hurt of denying the very Son of God. He walked alone on the hillsides, weeping in pain and sorrow. Those bitter tears worked a sweet miracle in him. He then shook Satan's kingdom.

We do not fight against enemies of flesh and blood; ours are more powerful! Our enemies are fear, rejection, bitterness, worry, loneliness, emptiness, guilt, depression, and despair. Do you want victory over all your enemies? Here are three suggestions: (1) learn to hunger for holiness and to hate your enemy—bitterness, rejection, etc.; (2) you must be convinced that God loves you in spite of your sin; (3) you must accept your Father's loving help in resisting and overcoming.

Chapter 12

CURSE-PROOF YOUR HOME

Is your home free from the curses Satan would like to bring upon your family? A famous family counselor and preacher once said, "Over 50 percent of families are divorcing and another 23 percent go to bed at night contemplating it." Thousands upon thousands of families are cursed with failure all over this earth. Family curses ignore race, professional status, and church preferences; and it leaves behind a terrible result of sin.

God truly must have been thinking of families when He said, "My people are destroyed for lack of knowledge" (Hosea 4:6). Satan is gaining victory in so many homes because of our own lack of knowledge. Remember, Satan is crafty and sneaky. He uses the most subtle devices and one of the most powerful is lack of understanding. Curse-proofing your home is a continuous and daily progressive lifestyle. You must first and foremost know Christ as your personal Lord and Savior.

Ask yourself these two questions: "If I were to die tonight would I go to heaven when Jesus comes?" and "If I stood at the gates of heaven and Jesus asked me why He should let me in, what would I say?" If you hesitate long on question number one or if you answer with, "I don't know," "I'm not sure," or "I hope so," then you're not protecting your home with the first prerequisite.

"These things have I written unto you that believe on the name of the Son of God; that ye may know that ye have eternal life, and that ye may believe on the name of the Son of God" (1 John 5:13).

"He that believeth on the Son hath everlasting life: and he that believeth not the Son shall not see life; but the wrath of God abideth on him" (John 3:36).

If you answer the second question with anything about your own works—what you have done—or about your deserving to be let in, then you are bringing a curse to your family instead of blessings.

"If you confess with your mouth the Lord Jesus and believe in your heart that God has raised Him from the dead, you will be saved. For with the heart one believes unto righteousness, and with the mouth confession is made unto salvation" (Rom. 10:9, 10, NKJV).

You must first see that heaven is a gift and nobody deserves it or can ever earn it. Yet, by faith we can believe it, and you should see the results of that faith in your life.

"There is a way that seems right to a man, but its end is the way of death" (Prov. 14:12, NKJV).

"There is no more important field of effort than that committed to the founders and guardians of the home. No work entrusted to human beings involves greater or more far-reaching results than does the work of fathers and mothers" (*The Ministry of Healing*, p. 350).

When parents who have devoted themselves to God start praying for their family and keeping them before God, blessings will come. Abraham prayed for the families in Sodom and Gomorrah. Though only Lot and some of his family were saved, Abraham did not give up praying for those two cities.

Prayer Breaks Curses

"Someone once told me about a Spirit-filled man whom I'll call Tom. He had been praying for his sister who was hooked on drugs and involved in all kinds of immorality. She lived a very sinful life. One weekend, while their mother was away, the sister went out and didn't come home until 6:30 the next morning. She brought some athletic-looking guy home with her, and they went into her mother's bedroom.

"Tom was almost overwhelmed. He asked God what to do and was told, 'Throw the guy out!' He went into his mother's bedroom, told his sister to put her clothes on, and asked her boyfriend, 'How would you feel if your sister brought some guy home to sleep with her in your mother's bed? Would you like it?' The boyfriend responded, 'No.' Tom told him to get dressed and leave, and the guy did just that. His sister was absolutely furious.

"When Tom left and returned to school, he began to Satan-proof his sister. He stood in the gap and spoke *for* his sister saying, 'Satan, you can't have any part of my sister. Drugs, you can't have any part of my sister.' The work of God had cut through all the junk in her life and had turned her completely around" (Marilyn Hickey, *Satan-Proof Your Home*, p. 21).

Bible Study Breaks Curses

When Jesus was being attacked by Satan He used Scripture to keep from falling to Satan's attacks. You know that Jesus' answer was, "It is written," right? When you find sin in your home or struggles in your home, you must have Scripture to claim over it with the faith of a mustard seed.

What if the curse of adultery has invaded your home, even just in thought? Pray the Scriptures: "Marriage is honorable among all, and the bed undefiled; but fornicators and adulterers God will judge" (Heb. 13:4, NKJV). Is there arguing in your home? Claim that God will give you good, right words. Then claim a Bible verse about it.

"How forceful are right words! But what does your arguing prove?" (Job 6:25, NKJV).

"Pleasant words are like a honeycomb, sweetness to the soul and health to the bones" (Prov. 16:24, NKJV).

> **IF YOU WANT TO CURSE-PROOF YOUR HOME, YOU MUST FELLOWSHIP WITH OTHERS WHO WANT TO PROTECT THEIR HOMES AND COMMUNITIES.**

Do you have a home with rebellious children? Is there selfishness and greed in your home? Place Scripture as the blessing to your home. "Thus says the Lord: Refrain your voice from weeping, and your eyes from tears; for your work shall be rewarded, says the LORD, and they shall come back from the land of the enemy" (Jer. 31:16, NKJV).

Other Tools for Curse-Proofing Your Home

If you want to curse-proof your home, you must fellowship with others who want to protect their homes and communities. The wrong people can cause more danger to your family than you might think.

"Then God blessed them, and God said to them, 'Be fruitful and multiply; fill the earth and subdue it; have dominion over the fish of the sea, over the birds of the air, and over every living thing that moves on the earth' " (Gen. 1:28, NKJV).

"For I have known him, in order that he may command his children and his household after him, that they keep the way of the LORD, to do righteousness and justice, that the LORD may bring to Abraham what He has spoken to him" (Gen. 18:19, NKJV).

Fellowship with families who want God's blessings on the earth and who will teach their children and will encourage your children to be followers of Christ.

You must also worship in God's house. This brings protection to your home. Find a church that keeps all of the commandments of God, holds communion, and practices baptism by immersion. (These last two ordinances are commissioned in Scripture.)

"I was glad when they said to me, 'Let us go into the house of the LORD' " (Ps.122:1, NKJV).

"Not forsaking the assembling of ourselves together, as the manner of some is; but exhorting one another" (Heb. 10:25).

You can be free from generational curses today by the blood of Jesus! You can turn around the curses, causing them to become blessings that will continue for "a thousand generations!"

"… greater is He who is in you than he who is in the world" (1 John 4:4, NKJV).

Bibliography

Hickey, Marilyn. *Breaking Generational Curses*, Tulsa, Okla: Harrison House Publishers, 2001.

Hickey, Marilyn. *Satan-Proof Your Home*, Tulsa, Okla: Marilyn Hickey Ministries, 1995.

Loritts Jr., Crawford. "Men of Action." *Promise Keepers Quarterly Report*, January 1996.

White, E. G. *The Acts of the Apostles*. Mountain View, CA: Pacific Press Publ. Assn., 1911.

———. *The Adventist Home*. Hagerstown, MD: Review and Herald Publ. Assn., 1952.

———. *The Desire of Ages*. Mountain View, CA: Pacific Press Publ. Assn., 1898.

———. "Disease and Its Causes." *The Review and Herald*, July 4, 1899.

———. *Christ's Object Lessons*. Review and Herald Publishing Association, 1900.

———. *Fundamentals of Christian Education*. Nashville, TN: Southern Publ. Assn., 1923.

———. *The Ministry of Healing.* Mountain View, CA: Pacific Press Publ. Assn., 1905.

———. *Patriarchs and Prophets.* Washington, D.C.: Review and Herald Publ. Assn., 1890.

———. *Prophets and Kings.* Mountain View, CA: Pacific Press Publ. Assn., 1917.

———. *Testimonies for the Church*, vol. 1. Mountain View, CA: Pacific Press Publ. Assn., 1885.

———. *Testimonies for the Church*, vol. 2. Mountain View, CA: Pacific Press Publ. Assn., 1885.

———. *Testimonies for the Church*, vol. 3. Mountain View, CA: Pacific Press Publ. Assn., 1885.

———. *Testimonies for the Church*, vol. 4. Mountain View, CA: Pacific Press Publ. Assn., 1885.

———. *Testimonies for the Church*, vol. 7. Mountain View, CA: Pacific Press Publ. Assn., 1902.

TEACH Services, Inc.
P U B L I S H I N G

We invite you to view the complete
selection of titles we publish at:
www.TEACHServices.com

We encourage you to write us
with your thoughts about this,
or any other book we publish at:
info@TEACHServices.com

TEACH Services' titles may be purchased in
bulk quantities for educational, fund-raising,
business, or promotional use.
bulksales@TEACHServices.com

Finally, if you are interested in seeing
your own book in print, please contact us at:
publishing@TEACHServices.com

We are happy to review your manuscript at no charge.

www.ingramcontent.com/pod-product-compliance
Lightning Source LLC
Chambersburg PA
CBHW070543170426
43200CB00011B/2536

LIKE FATHER

LIKE SON

LIKE GRANDSON

Curse-Proofing Your Family and Home

The Mystery of Exodus 20:5
"I the LORD thy God am a jealous God,
visiting the iniquity of the fathers
upon the children unto the third and fourth generation…"

Mitch Elrod

TEACH Services, Inc.
P U B L I S H I N G
www.TEACHServices.com • (800) 367-1844

World rights reserved. This book or any portion thereof may not be copied or reproduced in any form or manner whatever, except as provided by law, without the written permission of the publisher, except by a reviewer who may quote brief passages in a review.

The author assumes full responsibility for the accuracy of all facts and quotations as cited in this book. The opinions expressed in this book are the author's personal views and interpretations, and do not necessarily reflect those of the publisher.

This book is provided with the understanding that the publisher is not engaged in giving spiritual, legal, medical, or other professional advice. If authoritative advice is needed, the reader should seek the counsel of a competent professional.

Copyright © 2025 Mitch Elrod
Copyright © 2025 TEACH Services, Inc.
Published in Calhoun, Georgia, USA
ISBN-13: 978-1-4796-1772-2 (Paperback)
ISBN-13: 978-1-4796-1773-9 (ePub)
Library of Congress Control Number: 2024916555

All scripture quotations, unless otherwise indicated, are taken from King James Version. Public domain.

Scripture quotations marked GW are taken from God's Word, Copyright © 1995, 2003, 2013, 2014, 2019, 2020 by God's Word to the Nations Mission Society. Used by permission.

All Scripture references marked NET are taken from the New English Translation of the Bible, NET Bible®, copyright © 1996–2017 by Biblical Studies Press, L.L.C. http://netbible.com. All rights reserved.

All Scripture references marked NIV are taken from the Holy Bible, New International Version®, NIV®, copyright © 1973, 1978, 1984, 2011 by Biblica, Inc.®. Used by permission. All rights reserved worldwide.

All Scripture references marked NKJV are taken from the New King James Version® of the Bible, copyright © 1982 by Thomas Nelson. Used by permission. All rights reserved.